DEDICATION

To the glory of God.
In memory of my father, Carl E. Pelander; in honor of my mother, Isabelle Pelander;
and with thanks and praise for my husband Richard, daughters Rebecca and Beverly, and brother Dan,
who have been a continual source of love and encouragement.

— Nancy Pelander Johnson

This book is dedicated to my precious children, Jonathen, Jessica, and J.J.,
three beautiful gifts from a loving Heavenly Father. May children of all ages
appreciate the beauty and diversity of the animals in this book, but more
importantly see the awesome power of God reflected in their creation.

— Lloyd R. Hight

ACKNOWLEDGEMENTS

With many thanks to David Jolly, Ken Ham, and the staff of Answers in Genesis for
time and energy spent proofing and editing this book. Their valuable insight and
assistance has enhanced the quality of information to benefit our young readers.

CONTENTS

INTRODUCTION

God Created the Animals

In the Book of Genesis (the first book of the Bible), God created the universe, the plants, and the animals:

"And God said, Let the waters bring forth abundantly the moving creature that hath life, and fowl that may fly above the earth in the open firmament of heaven" (Genesis 1:20).

God created other animals also:

"And God said, Let the earth bring forth the living creature after his kind, cattle, and creeping thing, and beast of the earth after his kind: and it was so" (Genesis 1:24).

God saw this was good. After He made the animals, He created man and woman:

"And God said, Let us make man in our image, after our likeness: and let them have dominion over the fish of the sea, and over the fowl of the air, and over the cattle, and over all the earth, and over every creeping thing that creepeth upon the earth" (Genesis 1:26).

And God saw that all this was good. All animals were created on Day 5 and Day 6. Then man was created, also on Day 6. God gave to man dominion and rule over the animals.

Animals on the Ark

In Genesis 7:8, God told Noah to take every kind of land animal onto the ark so they would be saved from the Great Flood. God has a purpose for every animal He created, even the ones which seem dangerous to us. We must remember that in the beginning, God made animals for man's enjoyment, and animals ate only plants (Genesis 1:30). They did not kill each other. But sin changed this perfect creation. Not every animal God created is mentioned in the Bible, but in this book, we will look at 95 that are found in the Bible.

Animals: They Help Us in Many Ways

Animals are very important to us. After Adam sinned, we depended on them for wool and leather for clothing. After the Great Flood in the days of Noah, God gave us permission to eat their meat, which also meant we could eat eggs and drink animal milk. In some parts of the world people still depend on animals for transportation, just as people did in Bible times.

Some people depend on animals to make their living (cattle ranchers, shepherds, chicken farmers, dairy farmers, and fishermen). Others depend on animals, too. Textile companies use sheep's wool to make thread for fabric, other companies use cow and animal hides for leather products. These are just a few needs we have for animals. There are many more.

In biblical times, a person's wealth was measured by the number and kind of animals he owned. Clothes, rugs, and even tents were made from animal hair, and animal horns were also used for storage and drink containers.

The Hebrew Language

Some Bibles give different names for an animal. You may find a Bible verse that does not have the same animal name as an animal in this book. This can happen because the Bible was originally translated from the Hebrew language, and sometimes words in Hebrew don't translate easily into English.

In Bible times there were some animals mentioned that no longer exist today. Some of these animals are now called by different names. For example, we do not hear about the "leviathan" or "behemoth" anymore because the word "dinosaur" didn't exist until the nineteenth century.

Clean and Unclean Animals

In biblical times, there were no refrigerators or electric stoves. Food, especially meat, had to be handled and cooked carefully so it would not spoil. There were many laws about food, and God had certain rules He wanted His people to follow. Some animals were "clean" (they could be eaten), and some animals were "unclean" (they could not be eaten). This was an important law, because unclean animals could have caused people to become very ill.

Animals Given for Offering

In Bible times certain animals were used for sacrifice (offering) as a gift to God. Just as people give money in offering plates in churches, people of Bible times gave animals they owned for offerings. Four kinds of animals were given for offering: cattle, sheep, goats, and birds (doves and partridges).

Animals of the Bible

It is hoped the information in this book will be useful to you in learning about the animals that existed in Bible times. God created the animals to help His people, both in Bible times and today.

God cares for all His creation, and He especially cares for us. In the New Testament (John 21:15) Jesus refers to us as His "lambs" and His "sheep," and the Bible tells us He is our Shepherd (John 10:11).

INTRODUCTION

ADDER

The adder is a type of snake. It is part of the family of snakes called vipers. It is poisonous and its bite can be deadly. It is found throughout Europe, Asia, and Africa. It has a flat, triangle-shaped head and long, curved fangs. The adder can be black, grey, green, or brown — often with white spots.

The Bible tells us the adder's venom (or poison) is very strong. It hears by being sensitive to vibrations it feels from the ground.

The darker-colored adder has a zig-zag pattern of marks on its back.

The adder is sometimes called a viper, and in some versions of the Bible is called a cockatrice.

Their poison is like the poison of a serpent: they are like the deaf adder that stoppeth her ear (Psalm 58:4).

8

ANT

The ant is a tiny but wise creature. The Bible tells us this insect has no leader, but is a very busy worker. The ant collects food during the summer and then stores it for use during the winter.

Ants were common in Bible times as they are today. The black ant and the brown ant are the most common.

Ants live in groups called colonies, which are made up mostly of worker ants. The worker ants are female ants.

The queen ant lays the eggs, and the worker ants take care of the queen and the baby ants.

The Bible tells us that lazy people can learn a lesson from ants, because ants are hard workers.

Go to the ant, thou sluggard; consider her ways, and be wise: Which having no guide, overseer, or ruler, Provideth her meat in the summer, and gathereth her food in the harvest (Proverbs 6:6-8).

9

APE
(Primates)

Apes are mentioned twice in the Bible. They were not from Bible lands, but every three years, King Solomon's fleet of ships from Tarshish would come, bringing gold, silver, ivory, apes, and peacocks.

It is likely that there were more monkeys in Bible lands than apes (the two are of the same kind, but monkeys have long tails, while apes do not), and it has been said that monkeys were used as an article of trade for other items.

For the king had at sea a navy . . . bringing gold, and silver, ivory, and apes, and peacocks (1 Kings 10:22).

ASP

The asp is a snake similar to the cobra. The asp, like the cobra, is a poisonous snake. It is found in many parts of the world. This snake lives in a hole in the ground. Its venom (or poison) is fast-acting, and affects the nervous system of its victims. The asp eats small birds and toads.

This snake is a viper, as is the adder.

The Bible tells us that wicked people are like the asp, because they lie, and bad things which they say are as bad as the poison of the asp.

11

BADGER

The Bible tells us the badger is a wise animal. It is not big, but manages to make a home in the rocks.

The badger has short, strong legs, with toes made for burrowing in the ground. It looks like a weasel, and is nocturnal and hunts at night. The fur of a badger was valuable during Bible times. Its skin was used as an offering to God and was also used to make shoes and sandals.

Badgers eat gophers and other pests, and its face looks like a raccoon's. It is also a shy animal, but can be very powerful and vicious when cornered.

The conies [badgers] are but a feeble folk, yet make they their houses in the rocks (Proverbs 30:26).

BAT

In the Old Testament (Leviticus 11:19), the Bible tells us the bat was an unclean animal. An unclean animal was an animal that God did not want people to eat. The animals that were unclean most likely would have made people sick if they had eaten them.

In Bible lands, more than 20 types of bats have been found. Bats like dark places and live in caves. They are nocturnal animals, sleeping during the day, and flying out from their caves at night to search for food.

In flight, bats can be so thick in number that they seem to darken the sky.

God gave bats a radar system that allows them to find insects and fruit to eat, while also helping with direction. This radar is so complicated, only a Creator who knows everything could have designed it. This is another reason evolution can't be true!

Bats, in Bible times as well as today, are very helpful to the environment because they eat lots of insects that could destroy crops or carry disease.

BEAR

A bear can be a dangerous animal. Just as we are cautious of bears, people in Bible times, and especially shepherds, had to watch out for bears. Bears were dangerous because they could attack flocks of sheep, and even shepherds. They were thought of as vicious and destructive animals.

An evil person or ruler in Bible times was often compared to a bear. In Old Testament times there lived a shepherd named David. The Bible tells us he would kill any bear that would try to attack the sheep in his flock. David was just a boy, but was a fierce fighter, and he knew God would help him keep his sheep safe.

Some bears live in the woods and feed on fruit, honey, insects, or small animals. Others live in open plains, while polar bears live in a completely different environment where it's cold.

The feeding habits of bears can vary. Some are vegetarians, others eat meat *and* plants.

They growl when annoyed, and are very fierce if their cubs are taken away from them.

He was unto me as a bear lying in wait, and as a lion in secret places (Lamentations 3:10).

BEE

Bees were very important to people in Bible times. They provided honey, which was used as food, and also as a sweetener for cakes or other foods.

Honey was also used as a medicine to soothe sore throats (as it is still used today), and to put on cuts or wounds.

In Bible times people collected honey from wild honeycombs.

In the Old Testament Book of Exodus, God's people were promised they would be brought to "a land flowing with milk and honey." This meant the land would be a good place for them to live and would provide good soil for growing food.

Bees are nature's most important pollinating insect. They depend on pollen for protein and for nectar from flowers for energy. The pollen sticks to the bees' feet, and in this way they carry the pollen from one plant to the next. This enables the plants to produce flowers or fruit.

Bees can attack if their honeycomb is disturbed, and they will sting if they think something is annoying them.

BEETLE

The beetle is the largest order of insects in that there are about 250,000 different kinds of beetles in the world. They can grow as large as six inches long! The beetle has wings, but also spends time walking on the ground. Its wings look like a hardened shell. The hardened wings cover the beetle's abdomen when it is not flying.

In Old Testament times, people ate locusts, crickets, and grasshoppers; however, the Bible warned people not to eat any "small things that have wings and crawl," which included the beetle. It was thought of as an unclean animal.

Some Bibles use the word grasshopper or locust in place of beetle. This is due to a difference of meaning in translation from the Hebrew language.

All fowls that creep, going upon all four, shall be an abomination unto you. Yet these may ye eat of every flying creeping thing that goeth upon all four, which have legs above their feet, to leap withal upon the earth; Even these of them ye may eat; the locust after his kind, and the bald locust after his kind, and the beetle after his kind, and the grasshopper after his kind. But all other flying creeping things, which have four feet, shall be an abomination unto you (Leviticus 11:20-23).

BEHEMOTH

Behold now behemoth, which I made with thee; he eateth grass as an ox. Lo now, his strength is in his loins, and his force is in the navel of his belly (Job 40:15-16).

The behemoth is mentioned in the Bible, and comes from the word "beheman," meaning "beast."

The Bible tells us about the behemoth in the Book of Job 40:15-24. The behemoth eats grass "like an ox," and has great strength in its body. It also has powerful muscles, a stiff tail as strong as a cedar (a hardwood tree), and has legs of great strength. The behemoth stayed among thorn bushes and in reeds of swamps and marshes. It was a brave animal and not afraid of danger.

We know the dinosaur very well matches the description of the behemoth, because it was a very large animal with a body of great strength. It had bones "like bronze" and limbs "like bars of iron."

It is believed dinosaurs became extinct sometime after the Great Flood. We don't know what caused the extinction, but some of the theories include disease, harsher climate, loss of food supply, and being hunted by man.

BIRDS

There are many places in the Bible that tell us about birds. Genesis 1 tells us that birds were created on Day 5. Also in the Book of Genesis (the first book in the Bible), there is a story about a man named Noah. God told Noah there would be a Great Flood, and that he should build an ark, which was a special kind of large boat. God told Noah to take every kind of animal and every kind of bird with him onto the ark. It was a bird (a dove) that found dry land for Noah after the flood waters went down.

The Bible also tells us about birds that could and could not be eaten in the Old Testament Book of Leviticus.

In Bible times birds were caught in snares or nets. We also know from the Bible that God provides for the birds, just as he provides food, shelter, and warmth for us.

Other words in the Bible which refer to birds are: "fowls of the air," "fowls of heaven," or "feathered fowl."

Birds range in size from the bee hummingbird, to the ostrich. The smallest and largest extinct birds are the moa and elephant bird.

They, and every beast after his kind, and all the cattle after their kind, and every creeping thing that creepeth upon the earth after his kind, and every fowl after his kind, every bird of every sort (Genesis 7:14).

CAMEL

The camel was a very important animal in Bible times. They provided transportation, were used for carrying heavy loads, and were also used in calvary. The camel is not an easy animal to ride, because its swaying motion can cause motion sickness.

The camel is a good desert traveler, and walks at a speed of about 10 miles per hour. The Arabian camel can travel more than 100 miles per day.

The camel has cushioned feet that do not sink into the sand. Its hump is made of a sponge-like tissue, where it stores its food. Camels can travel a long way without water, and can go for up to one week without a drink. The camel stores water in its stomach.

The camel has long eyelashes to protect their eyes from sand, and can also close its nostrils to keep out blowing sand. These are wonderful signs that God designed camels to function exactly as they need to function in their particular environment.

In Bible times, the man who owned many camels was a wealthy person. And, we're told in the Bible that John the Baptist wore a coat of camel hair.

And he entreated Abram well for her sake: and he had sheep, and oxen, and she [donkeys], and menservants, and maidservants, and she [donkeys], and camels (Genesis 12:16).

CANKERWORM

Cankerworm is a common name for caterpillars known as "inchworms." Inchworms feed from plants and trees by chewing off the leaves.

The cankerworm is an insect mentioned by prophets in the Bible. It was actually an insect called the locust, which looks like a grasshopper. These insects caused much damage to crops. The locust was also used for food.

When the cankerworm is young, it looks like a caterpillar. When it gets bigger, it enters a cocoon and transforms into a locust.

And I will restore to you the years that the locust hath eaten, the cankerworm, and the caterpillar, and the palmerworm, my great army which I sent among you (Joel 2:25).

CATERPILLAR

In the Bible the caterpillar refers to a stage of development of the locust (which is like a grasshopper).

He gave also their increase unto the caterpillar, and their labour unto the locust (Psalm 78:46).

When the locust is still a larvae (after it is hatched), it looks like a caterpillar. It ruins crops and other plants by chewing on them. When it gets bigger, it enters a cocoon and transforms into a locust. (Also see Cankerworm.)

CATTLE

Cattle are mentioned hundreds of times in the Bible, and were an important animal to people in those days.

Owning cattle was a sign of great wealth, and the more cattle a man owned, the more wealthy he was. Cattle were used for working in the fields to thresh grain, and were used for food (beef). Most farmers could not afford cattle, and often they would buy a donkey to do the work instead, which cost less.

Cattle in Bible times were, for the most part, more wild-looking than they are today. They were most likely shaggy-looking, and roamed about as they pleased.

In the winter, cattle were "fattened" to gain weight so they would provide better meat for eating.

Cattle were fed fodder, which means cattle feed. This was usually barley. Cattle were also fed straw or beans. They were usually fed in stalls rather than in the pasture.

The Bible tells us that Adam named the animals which God created, including cattle. In Psalm 50:10 God reminds us that the animals and cattle belong to Him.

And God made the beast of the earth after his kind, and cattle after their kind, and every thing that creepeth upon the earth after his kind: and God saw that it was good (Genesis 1:25).

22

CHAMELEON

The chameleon is a type of lizard (a reptile), and was considered one of the "unclean" animals. The Old Testament tells us that certain creatures were unclean, and were forbidden as food.

The chameleon is a small lizard (perhaps reaching a length of over a foot long), and it protects itself by changing color. It will turn green if it stays in a grassy or tree-filled environment, and it will turn brown if living in rocks, sand, or desert.

There are more than 80 types of chameleons. This animal has a very short neck, and a head that does not turn. Instead, its eyes move separately from each other, enabling it to see from side to side. It also has a very long tongue, which helps it catch its prey.

And the ferret, and the chameleon, and the lizard, and the snail, and the mole (Leviticus 11:30).

CHICKEN

In Bible times people raised chickens for meat and eggs (just as they do today). Chickens were sold at local meat markets, and eggs were gathered, not only from chickens, but from other wild fowl as well. Eggs were probably eaten often, just as they are today.

Just as a hen gathers baby chicks under her wings to protect them, in the Bible God tells us how much He cares for us.

In the Bible, God often uses examples of animals to show us how precious we are to Him. Here, God is telling us that as our loving parent, He will protect us from harm.

O Jerusalem, Jerusalem, thou that killest the prophets, and stonest them which are sent unto thee, how often would I have gathered thy children together, even as a hen gathereth her chickens under her wings, and ye would not! (Matthew 23:37).

COCK

Jesus said unto him, "Verily I say unto thee, That this night, before the cock crow, thou shalt deny me thrice" (Matthew 26:34).

A cock and a rooster are the same animal. The Bible verse from Matthew 26:34 tells us the words of Jesus to His follower, Simon Peter.

Before Jesus was arrested and crucified (hung on the Cross to die), He told Simon Peter that before the cock (rooster) was to crow that night, that Simon Peter would say three times to the enemy that he did not know Jesus. Even though he really did know Jesus, Simon Peter lied to keep himself from being harmed.

Jesus knew ahead of time that Simon Peter would lie. Jesus knew He would have to die on the Cross to save us from our sins.

A cock or rooster is a male chicken. The rooster crows at dawn, letting everyone know that the day has begun.

CONY

The cony is a hoofed animal, found in Africa and the Middle East. It has a thick body, short legs, a pointed face, and rounded ears. The cony is known by other names: rock hyrax, rock badger, or rock rabbit. It is the size of a large rabbit, but looks like a guinea pig.

The cony is about 20 inches long, has hooflike claws, and soft pads on the bottom of its feet for climbing. It has molar-type teeth which are similar to teeth of the rhinoceros.

The Old Testament tells us that any land animal that has a divided hoof and chews the cud could be eaten; however, the cony chews the cud, but does not have a divided hoof, so it was considered unclean and not to be eaten.

The cony can live either in trees or on the ground, but most live on the ground among the rocks. They eat leaves and branches of plants, and are nocturnal, searching for food at night. If bothered, the cony can send out a strong odor like a skunk.

The Bible tells us the cony is a wise animal: "The conies are but a feeble folk, yet they make their houses in the rocks"(Proverbs 30:26).

And the cony, because he cheweth the cud, but divideth not the hoof; he is unclean to you (Leviticus 11:5).

CORMORANT

The cormorant is a web-footed water bird. It is also a fish-eating bird, and is found along seacoasts around the world. These birds like tropical climates, which are warm.

The cormorant is a large bird with a long neck and slender beak. Usually it is black. To catch fish, the cormorant dives under water. It makes its nest in rocky areas of the coast. It is a common bird in the area of the Mediterranean Sea.

And these are they which ye shall have in abomination among the fowls; they shall not be eaten . . . the little owl, and the cormorant, and the great owl (Leviticus 11:13-17).

COW
(also see "Cattle")

When talking about cattle, we need to understand that "cows" refer to females, while "bulls" refer to males.

Cows were used for sacrifice (offerings) to God during Old Testament times. A sacrifice in those days meant that a person was giving a gift to God, just as today we give money gifts to God in the offering plate at church.

The Bible tells us cows were trained to thresh grain, and they were used for milking.

In Old Testament times, there was a man named Jacob. He gave his brother Esau a gift of many animals, including cows.

But the firstling of a cow, or the firstling of a sheep, or the firstling of a goat, thou shalt not redeem; they are holy: thou shalt sprinkle their blood upon the altar, and shalt burn their fat for an offering made by fire, for a sweet savour unto the Lord (Numbers 18:17).

CRANE

The crane is a tall bird, much like a stork. It is the largest type of wading bird. It has a long neck and a long, straight beak. It is sometimes gray with a black head, and has a red patch on top, but the majority of cranes are mostly white. Its wings are short, but powerful, and it migrates to Bible lands each year.

The distinctive voice of the crane can be heard from far away. The Bible tells us the crane is a chattering bird (Isaiah 38:14).

The crane eats small animals and grains. It likes being in and around water.

Like a crane or a swallow, so did I
chatter: I did mourn as a dove:
mine eyes fail with looking upward:
O Lord, I am oppressed; undertake
for me (Isaiah 38:14).

CUCKOO

Cuckoos have sharp-pointed beaks, and vary in size.

The cuckoo lives mostly in trees, and it feeds on caterpillars.

The mother cuckoo seems lazy. She lays her eggs in the nests of other birds instead of building one herself. The young baby cuckoo takes over the food in the nest, and then kicks out the babies that were originally there.

The cuckoo is mentioned in two books of the Bible: Leviticus 11:16 and Deuteronomy 14:15. It is listed as one of the unclean birds, and was not to be eaten.

*And the owl, and the night hawk, and
the cuckow [cuckoo], and the hawk
after his kind* (Deuteronomy 14:15).

DEER

And Solomon's provision for one day was thirty measures of fine flour, and three-score measures of meal, Ten fat oxen, and twenty oxen out of the pastures, and an hundred sheep, beside harts, and roebucks, and fallowdeer, and fatted fowl (1 Kings 4:22-23).

There are a number of different types of deer mentioned in the Bible. They are: the hart, the hind, the fallow deer, and the roe or roebuck.

In Old Testament times, there was once a wise and wealthy king named Solomon. God was pleased with King Solomon and gave him much wisdom. He had a very large kingdom, and needed many supplies each day for meals. The Bible tells us in 1 Kings 4:22 that King Solomon needed deer and roebuck each day to help provide food for the many people in his kingdom, so we know deer were often hunted in Bible times.

DOG

Give not that which is holy unto the dogs, neither cast ye your pearls before swine, lest they trample them under their feet, and turn again and rend you (Matthew 7:6).

In Bible times dogs were not always the friendly animals that they are today. Instead, they often roamed village streets in search of food, which they would find in garbage piles. They were fierce and hungry, and would often run wild.

People in Bible times did not like dogs very much, except for watch dogs or sheep dogs, which were used to protect flocks of sheep from dangerous predators.

Jesus tells us in Matthew 7: "Do not give what is holy to dogs — they will only turn and attack you." Something that is holy is sacred, from God.

There is also a story in the Bible about a woman's daughter who was ill. She asked Jesus for help. Jesus said, "It is not fair to take the children's bread and throw it to the dogs." And the woman answered, "Yes, Lord, yet even the dogs eat the crumbs that fall from their master's table." Jesus then said, "O woman, great is your faith!" And He healed the woman's daughter instantly.

On Day 6 of creation, God created dogs, but really just one kind of dog, from which we get various breeds of dogs today. There are variations of dogs, such as wolves and coyotes, but just one dog (kind).

DONKEY

People rode donkeys and often used them as pack animals to carry heavy loads in Bible times. Most farmers owned a donkey to work plows, corn mills, or water wheels. The donkey was also much cheaper than other work animals. Sometimes the donkey was paired with an ox to do the work. Donkeys are sure-footed animals and can easily climb rocky areas. They usually have a white muzzle and underparts, and most have a black stripe which runs down their back. Donkeys eat hay, and also like raw vegetables and breads. Donkeys also need salt, which they eat from a salt block.

Donkeys are usually ridden when they are about two and a half years old, and at age one and a half they can carry light loads.

Burro is the Spanish word for donkey. In the southwestern part of the United States, donkeys are often called burros.

Mary rode on a donkey to Bethlehem with Joseph before Jesus was born. Before Jesus was crucified, He rode a donkey through the town of Jerusalem, where people laid out their coats and palm branches onto the street before Him, in His honor.

The Bible tells us other things about donkeys. They were made to rest, and not work, on the Sabbath Day (the day of worship). They know their owner well, and God cares for them.

And Jesus, when he had found a young [donkey], sat thereon; as it is written, "Fear not, daughter of Zion: behold, thy King cometh, sitting on an [donkey's] colt" (John 12:14-15).

DOVE

The dove was the most important bird in Bible times. On the ark, Noah sent out a dove to find the first sign of land after the great waters of the flood had subsided.

Doves are found throughout the world. They are a member of the same group of birds as pigeons, but are smaller. They stay on the ground or in trees, and they eat seeds, fruit, and insects. Doves can fly great distances. They make a cooing sound. They often live in nests and bushes.

Doves were used in Bible times for sacrifice (offering) at the altar. These birds were kept in large numbers in the temples because they were used so often for sacrifice.

The dove is a symbol for the Holy Spirit. It is a gentle bird, and represents the gentleness of Jesus. The Holy Spirit is the comforter that God promised He would send to us for help.

And I said, Oh that I had wings like a dove! for then would I fly away, and be at rest (Psalm 55:6).

DRAGON

In the Bible the dragon is a symbol for sin and for satan (the devil), although there are several references to real creatures, probably some type of dinosaur. The legend of the dragon makes us think of a huge scaly creature with wings, large claws, and a fiery breath.

And Babylon shall become heaps, a dwellingplace for dragons, an astonishment, and an hissing, without an inhabitant (Jeremiah 51:37).

The Bible tells us in various verses what the dragon is like: often a red color, powerful, and found in the wilderness, deserted cities, and dry places.

The word "dinosaur" was not invented until about 100 years ago, so it doesn't appear in the Bible. However, we know from the use of words such as dragon, behemoth, and leviathan that the biblical references were to real creatures.

The dragon is a symbol of wicked people, and in the Bible both Pharaoh and Satan were very wicked.

EAGLE

Who satisfieth thy mouth with good things;
so that thy youth is renewed like the eagle's
(Psalm 103:5).

From ancient times eagles have been thought of as strong and brave birds. The eagle has sturdy legs and feet, as it has long toes with curved claws, called talons.

The eagle is a swift bird. It can fly at very high altitudes, where it builds nests in high places that cannot be easily reached.

In Bible times the eagle was a symbol of great faith, since it's a bird that was so well thought of: strong, brave, and good to its young.

The eagle lives in high rocky mountain areas. It carefully trains and cares for its young. The eagle catches its young on its wings when teaching the babies to fly. This way they are protected from falling from great heights before they can fly easily on their own.

There are a number of places in the Bible which tell about the swiftness (quickness) of the eagle.

In the Old Testament, we find the eagle was a bird that was not to be eaten. The bald eagle is pictured on the Great Seal of the United States. For Americans, it is a symbol of strength and courage, just as it was to people in Bible times.

EWE

The rich man had exceeding many flocks and herds: But the poor man nothing, save one little ewe lamb, which he had bought and nourished up: and it grew up together with him, and with his children; it did eat of his own meat, and drank of his own cup, and lay in his bosom, and was unto him as a daughter (2 Samuel 12:2-3).

A ewe is a female sheep. Ewes were sometimes used for sacrifice in Old Testament times, and only the ewes without "blemish" (the most perfect ones) could be used as an offering to God.

The Bible tells us in 2 Samuel 12:2-3 that poor people owned perhaps only one ewe lamb. The rich people owned many flocks and herds of sheep, and the more animals they owned, the more wealthy they were.

37

FERRET

The ferret is a type of weasel, and in Old Testament times it was thought of as an unclean animal, and was not to be eaten.

The ferret has red eyes, and its fur is usually yellow or white. It is sensitive to the cold, and must be kept warm if not living in the wild.

The ferret is sometimes used for rabbit hunting or for killing rats.

Because the Bible is translated from the Hebrew language, sometimes people find more than one meaning for the word ferret. In some versions of the Bible, hedgehog is used instead of ferret. This is an example of an animal reference that we can't be sure of, since the word might have changed meanings.

And the ferret, and the chameleon, and the lizard, and the snail, and the mole (Leviticus 11:30).

FISH

Again, the kingdom of heaven is like unto a net, that was cast into the sea, and gathered of every kind: Which, when it was full, they drew to shore, and sat down, and gathered the good into vessels, but cast the bad away (Matthew 13:47-48).

The fish is a symbol of Jesus Christ. The early Christians (people who followed Christ) in Jesus' time used the fish as a symbol of their faith. The Greek word for fish is ichthys, and the Greek letters for fish mean Jesus Christ, Son of God, Saviour.

Jesus spoke about fish in many of the parables, or stories, that He told. One miracle Jesus performed was turning two fish and five loaves of bread into enough food to feed 5,000 people. Another miracle Jesus performed was to make a coin appear in a fish's mouth. He did this to show Peter, His disciple, that it was right to pay the temple tax owed to the tax collectors. He told Peter to go to the lake and throw in a fishing line. He was to pull in the first fish he hooked, which he did, and in the fish's mouth was a gold coin.

Fish were very plentiful in the Bible lands, which were surrounded by large areas of water. Many people ate fish, because there was so much of it, and meat was expensive.

Fish were roasted on an open fire. In the Book of John it says Jesus prepared fish this way.

Many followers of Jesus were fishermen. Jesus told them He wanted them to be "fishers of men." He wanted them to tell others about God.

FLEA

The flea is a tiny insect without wings. They are parasites, which means that they live on the skin of other animals. They suck the blood from the animal, and that becomes their food.

Fleas have oblong bodies and long legs. Their strong legs enable them to jump very high.

In Bible times, fleas were a nuisance to people and animals, just as they are to us today.

After whom is the king of Israel come out? after whom dost thou pursue? after a dead dog, after a flea (1 Samuel 24:14).

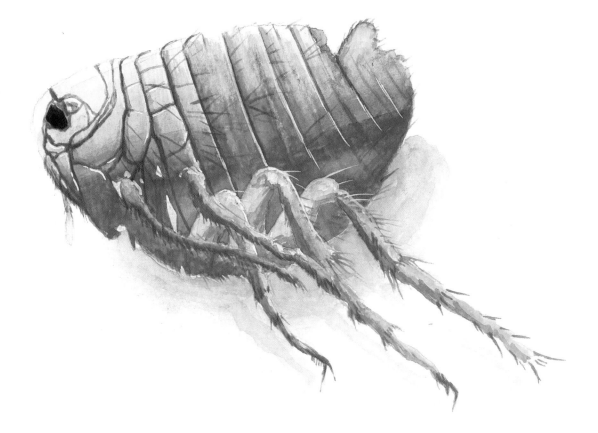

Else, if thou wilt not let my people go, behold, I will send swarms of flies upon thee, and upon thy servants, and upon thy people, and into thy houses: and the houses of the Egyptians shall be full of swarms of flies, and also the ground whereon they are (Exodus 8:21).

FLY

The fly is a two-winged insect. There are about 80,000 different types of flies, and they can be found throughout the world. They like warm places. They have six legs, and can cling to almost any surface. For example, this is why a fly can walk upside-down on the ceiling.

Flies destroy crops, and also carry diseases. In Bible times, God sent swarms of flies onto the people of Egypt, because they would not let Moses and his people (called the Israelites) out of the country.

In the Book of Ecclesiastes, the Bible tells us that dead flies cause a bad odor.

FOWL

In the Bible, the "birds of the air" are called fowl. Sometimes they are also called "fowls of the air," "fowls of heaven," or "feathered fowl."

God reminds us that all of creation belongs to him: "I know all the birds of the air, and all that moves in the field is mine" (Psalm 50:11).

In 1 Kings 4:33, the Bible tells us that King Solomon had great knowledge of birds, as well as reptiles, fish, and other animals. King Solomon was a wise man, and God gave him much knowledge. People came from many countries to hear King Solomon speak about the many things he knew.

Of every clean beast thou shalt take to thee by sevens, the male and his female: and of beasts that are not clean by two, the male and his female. Of fowls also of the air by sevens, the male and the female; to keep seed alive upon the face of all the earth (Genesis 7:2-3).

FOX

And Jesus saith unto him, "The foxes have holes, and the birds of the air have nests; but the Son of man hath not where to lay his head" (Matthew 8:20).

The fox is the smallest member of the dog family, canidae. The fox has thick fur, triangle-shaped ears, and a long, bushy tail. They are fast runners and can reach a speed of 30 miles per hour.

In Bible times, foxes were trouble-some. They caused much damage to vineyards (where grapes were grown). Special watchtowers were built in the vineyards to keep foxes away, because they liked to eat grapes. They also liked to eat animals, birds, and other fruit.

The Bible tells us foxes are found in deserts and live in holes.

Foxes are known to be crafty or sly, meaning they are tricky animals.

FROG

In Old Testament times, there was a man with the title Pharaoh, who was a king. He tried to keep the people of Moses in his country, and he would not let them leave. God told Moses to give Pharaoh a message: if he did not let Moses' people go, God would send swarms of frogs onto the land.

The king would not listen to Moses, so God sent millions of frogs into the country. The frogs were everywhere, and even in people's beds. The Bible tells us about this in Psalm 105:30.

Frogs like to be in moist places where there is water. Their body absorbs water through their skin. Some frogs live in trees, but most live near water.

Frogs eat insects, worms, and spiders. The frog's tongue is covered with a sticky substance which helps them catch their prey.

Some frogs are edible, which means they can be eaten. People still eat frog legs, and they are served in some restaurants.

And the Lord spake unto Moses, Go unto Pharaoh, and say unto him, Thus saith the Lord, Let my people go, that they may serve me. And if thou refuse to let them go, behold, I will smite all thy borders with frogs (Exodus 8:1-2).

GAZELLE
(Roebuck)

And it shall be as the chased roe, and as a sheep that no man taketh up: they shall every man turn to his own people, and flee every one into his own land (Isaiah 13:14).

The gazelle is a type of antelope. It lives in the open plains, and it can run at a great speed. The male gazelle has long, slender horns which curve forward. The female gazelle may or may not have horns. The gazelle is a sand color, with a white underside, and white markings on its face.

The gazelle is a very graceful animal, and in the Song of Solomon, the Bible compares the beauty of the gazelle to the beauty of the love that a bride and groom have for each other.

In Bible times there was a king named Solomon, who had a large kingdom with many people. Each day he used the meat from many animals, including the gazelle, (or oryx as illustrated here) to feed the people in his kingdom.

GIER

The gier is a large bird which looks similar to an eagle. It has strong, thick legs, and large wings. When flying, it looks like a falcon. It is also known as the lammergeir (or bearded vulture), the Egyptian vulture, or the ossifrage. In the Book of Leviticus and in the Book of Deuteronomy in the Old Testament it is listed as an unclean bird, and was not to be eaten.

The Egyptian vulture, gier (lammergeir), and the ossifrage are all types of vultures. Vultures help keep down disease by eating dead animals. They locate these dead organisms by using a keen sense of smell.

And the pelican, and the gier eagle, and the cormorant (Deuteronomy 14:17).

GNAT

Ye blind guides, which strain at a gnat, and swallow a camel (Matthew 23:24).

A gnat is a biting, two-winged fly. It is quite small. These insects caused many problems for people in Bible times. Gnats would get into water and wine jugs, and people would have to strain the gnats out of their drinking containers, or drinking vessels, as they were called, before they could have any water or wine.

The words from the Bible in Matthew 23:24 are the words of Jesus. He was upset with the hypocrites — these were the people who said they believed in Jesus, but instead they were not truthful. Jesus called them "blind guides." A guide who could not see would not be useful. Also, if a person were to strain out a gnat from his drink, that would not be a difficult thing to do. Jesus uses the idea of the camel to show them their untruthfulness was a big problem.

GOAT

The goat was an important animal in Bible times. People sold goats for money, ate goat meat, drank goat's milk, and used goats as a sacrifice (offering) to God.

The more goats a man owned, the wealthier he was. Some people owned very large flocks of goats, numbering in the thousands.

Goats were sometimes a larger part of a shepherd's flock than his sheep. The goats were driven ahead of the sheep by the shepherd, and these animals were brought to pastures to eat. When wild, goats live in hilly, rocky country.

Goatskins had a number of uses. Wine bags were made from goatskins, and they were used for stuffing pillows (1 Samuel 19:13). People also made coats and rugs from goatskins.

Goat's milk was a favorite drink, and cheese and butter were made from the goat's milk.

In Bible times, goats were also given as presents.

The lambs are for thy clothing, and the goats are the price of the field (Proverbs 27:26).

GRASSHOPPER

Even these of them ye may eat; the locust after his kind, and the bald locust after his kind, and the beetle after his kind, and the grasshopper after his kind (Leviticus 11:22).

The grasshopper is a winged insect that hops, and in the Old Testament the Bible tells us it was all right for people to eat grasshoppers, because they were not an unclean animal. The grasshopper, cricket, and locust were all used as food in Bible times, and there were many of them living in the dry desert areas.

Grasshoppers are usually from one to five inches long. Some change color from green to brown, or from brown to green, depending on the season of the year and their surroundings. They make a "chirping" sound by rubbing their back legs against their body. Their eardrums are in a strange place — they are located on their abdomen (in the middle of their side), just behind their back legs.

Grasshoppers caused problems for farmers, as they still do today, as they destroy crops by chewing on them.

The Bible also tells us this insect is burdensome, lowly, and inferior.

HARE

The hare, a member of the rabbit family, is only mentioned twice in the Bible (once in the Book of Leviticus and once in the Book of Deuteronomy). The original Hebrew word used by Moses may actually refer to an animal that no longer exists, but the people who translated it into English used "hare" because that is what they thought it meant.

The hare is an unclean animal even though it chews the cud; it does not have a split hoof. Chewing the cud means that an animal chews its food, swallows it and digests it part-way in the stomach. Then the food is returned to the mouth where the animal chews it a second time and then swallows it to be digested the rest of the way in its stomach.

Hares are plentiful in the Bible lands, where there is much desert.

And the hare, because he cheweth the cud, but divideth not the hoof; he is unclean unto you (Leviticus 11:6).

Doth the hawk fly by thy wisdom, and stretch her wings toward the south (Job 39:26).

HAWK

The Bible tells us that the hawk is an unclean animal, and must not be eaten.

The hawk has a strong, curved beak, and powerful claws, called talons. It is carnivorous (meat-eating) and feeds on small rodents, reptiles, and insects. It also has a loud, piercing voice.

The hawk builds its nest on high ledges, or in the tops of trees, safe from predators.

In the Bible the hawk is a symbol of swiftness. It can fly very high and fast, and it also has excellent eyesight.

HERON

In the Old Testament Book of Leviticus, we are told the heron is a bird which is unclean, and was not to be used as food.

The heron is a tall wading bird that looks like a crane, but is smaller. It lives in swampy places and on mud banks. It is a bird that is found all over the world.

One of the best-known herons is called the great blue heron. The bird is three feet long, and when its wings are spread out, they reach almost six feet wide.

There are ten different types of heron in the Bible lands.

And the stork, the heron after her kind, and the lapwing, and the bat
(Leviticus 11:13-19).

52

HOOPOE
(or Lapwing)

The hoopoe (called lapwing in the King James Version of the Bible) is an old world bird. It was a sacred bird to the Egyptian people. To the Hebrew people of the Bible lands, it was an abomination (greatly disliked), because it was an unclean animal, and was thought of as a dirty and filthy bird. It does not sing, and belongs to a family of birds called "nonpasserina," which means they are not songbirds.

The hoopoe is a small bird with a long bill. It builds its nest in holes. It makes a loud "lapping" sound with its wings, and is mentioned twice in the Bible.

And the stork, and the heron after her kind, and the lapwing (Deuteronomy 14:18).

HORNET

The hornet is an insect with a powerful sting. It makes a large nest which looks like paper. The hornet makes the nest from partly digested fibers from plants, and mud. The hornet builds its nest in trees, rocks, or on buildings.

In Bible times the hornet was used by God as punishment. There is a story in the Bible (Exodus 23:28), where God sent hornets to drive out groups of people in the land who did not obey Him or worship Him. This made it safer for God's good people to live on the land without the bad people bothering them. In the Bible, God calls these people the Hivite, Canaanite, and Hittite peoples.

And I will send hornets before thee, which shall drive out the Hivite, Canaanite, and the Hittite from before thee (Exodus 23:28).

Lloyd R. Hight

That led them through the deep, as an horse in the wilderness, that they should not stumble? (Isaiah 63:13).

HORSE

In Bible times, horses were used mostly by kings and warriors in battle. They were also used to pull chariots, which were fancy two-wheeled carts in which kings and other important people would ride.

The horse became a symbol of power in Bible times, and it cost a lot of money to buy a horse, especially if it came with a chariot.

Horses are sure-footed animals, so they were good for battle; however, they could not be ridden in rocky places, because in Bible times there were no horseshoes to protect horses' feet.

In battle, horses were protected with armor, and they were prepared and trained for war. Often they were adorned (decorated) with bells on their necks.

The Bible tells us that horses were swifter than eagles, and they were also used for sending messages. King Solomon, a very wealthy king, had 4,000 stalls for horses and chariots.

HORSELEECH

The horseleech is a leech, which is a large blood-sucking worm. Leeches are parasites, which live off the skin of other animals. They live on land, in the sea, in ponds, rivers, and swamps.

Leeches were used by doctors to cure people of certain diseases. Leeches were placed on the diseased area of a sick person's body, and the leeches would begin to suck blood from that area of the skin. It was believed the leech would cure the patient by sucking out the "bad blood."

The horseleech eats earthworms, tadpoles, and small fishes. It is mentioned only once in the Bible.

The horseleech got its name because at one time they were very bothersome to horses that drank water from ponds or swamps. The leeches would attach to the horse's nose or mouth while drinking, so these leeches became known as horseleeches.

The horseleech hath two daughters crying, Give, give. There are three things that are never satisfied, yea, four things say not, It is enough (Proverbs 30:15a).

HYENA

And the wild beasts of the islands shall cry in their desolate houses, and dragons in their pleasant palaces: and her time is near to come, and her days shall not be prolonged (Isaiah 13:22).

In some Bibles the hyena is called a "wild beast." It is an animal which has the face of a dog, rounded ears like a koala bear, and has a body the shape of a leopard's.

The hyena is a predator, which means it eats other animals to survive. It hunts in packs at night, feeding on hoofed animals. It uses its powerful jaws to crush the bones of its prey.

The most well-known is the spotted, or laughing hyena. It is called this because of its cry, which sounds like a person laughing.

IBEX
(wild goats)

The ibex is a type of wild goat. It is a strong animal with a sturdy body and long legs. It lives in high rocky places. It is a brownish-gray color, and has large, curved horns. The ibex is a good jumper that can jump very long distances.

The ibex was hunted so much in the past that now there are laws to protect it from extinction.

The high hills are a refuge for the wild goats; and the rocks for the conies
(Psalm 104:18).

JACKAL

And wild beasts of the desert shall lie there; and their houses shall be full of doleful creatures; and owls shall dwell there, and satyrs shall dance there
(Isaiah 13:21).

The jackal is a type of wild dog. It is the size of a fox but looks like a wolf. It has a tan-colored coat, with a dark-tipped tail. It lives both on the plains and in the deserts. During the day it stays in its hole in the ground. It is a nocturnal animal, so it stays awake at night. During this time, it hunts in packs for food. It is carnivorous, feeding on other animals.

Jackals were very common in Bible times. Often they would roam the towns at night, disturbing the silence with their howling. The Bible tells us the jackals prefer to live in lonely or deserted places.

KITE

The kite is a bird with long, slender wings and a long tail that looks similar to a falcon. It is a scavenger, and eats leftover bits of dead animals.

The Bible tells us in the Book of Leviticus, that the kite is a bird that is unclean and not to be eaten. There is another Bible verse in Deuteronomy 14:13, which again tells us this bird is not fit for eating.

The kite builds its nests from twigs high in the trees. Sometimes it nests in trees just above the water.

The kite likes warm climates and is found throughout the world. Various kites are found in Bible lands, the most common being the black kite, the red kite, and the yellow-billed kite.

And the glede, and the kite, and the vulture after his kind (Deuteronomy 14:13).

So when they had dined, Jesus saith to Simon Peter, "Simon, son of Jonas, lovest thou me more than these?" He saith unto him, Yea, Lord; thou knowest that I love thee. He saith unto him, "Feed my lambs" (John 21:15).

LAMB

The Bible tells us Jesus is the "Lamb of God." There are many verses in the Bible which mention lambs.

The lamb is a young sheep. It is protected by the shepherd who cares for it. Just as there were shepherds in Bible times, today we still have shepherds who care for sheep. Shepherds today may dress differently than people in Bible times did, but their job is the same: they tend the sheep, they make sure the sheep are well-fed, safe, and protected from predators.

Jesus is a shepherd to us, and we are His sheep. He is loving and caring, and He watches over us, just as a shepherd watches over his flocks.

In the Book of John (John 21:15) in the New Testament, Jesus reminds His disciples to "feed my lambs." By this He meant that they should go and tell God's people everywhere the good news, that Jesus is their Lord and Saviour.

LEOPARD

A leopard is a member of the cat family, felidae. It is large, being about four feet long. It is tan-colored and has black spots. Some leopards are completely black; they are called "black panthers."

There were once a lot of leopards living in the Bible lands, but there are fewer today because of the number of people who have hunted them.

The leopard is a good climber, and can even climb trees to hunt its prey.

The Bible tells us the leopard is carnivorous, is fierce, and swift. It lives in mountainous areas, and watches and waits to attack its prey.

The wolf also shall dwell with the lamb, and the leopard shall lie down with the kid; and the calf and the young lion and the fatling together; and a little child shall lead them (Isaiah 11:6).

LEVIATHAN

Canst thou draw out leviathan with an hook? or his tongue with a cord which thou lettest down? (Job 41:1).

In the Bible the leviathan is described as a large marine reptile, and very fierce. Some Bible verses refer to it as a whale or serpent, as it appears to have lived in water, but on closer study, we see that the description doesn't fit either a whale or a serpent.

In the Old Testament Book of Job (Job 41:15-17) there are clues which show the Leviathan as a giant dragon-like reptile: "His scales are his pride, shut up together as a close seal; one is so near to another, that no air can come between them; they are joined one to another, they stick together, that they cannot be sundered [broken]."

The Bible also tells us the leviathan was created by God, and that God had power over this great and strong creature.

The leviathan is said to have had "fearsome teeth," with the ability to shoot sparks or fire from its mouth and smoke could pour from its nostrils. It was a creature "without fear," and not approachable by even the bravest man.

The leviathan, just like some other huge creatures, is believed to have become extinct sometime after the Great Flood.

63

LION

The lion is mentioned a number of times in the Bible. Lions are a strong and proud animal. They are fierce, have much courage, and are not afraid of man. Lions have powerful legs, a large head, and a long, muscular body. It often takes its food back into the den (its home), where it eats and cares for its cubs.

In Bible times, robbers were often thrown to hungry lions, where they would be eaten. There is a story in the Bible about a man named Daniel, who worked for King Darius. Daniel was a good man and believed in God very much. A few men in the kingdom thought Daniel had broken the law, so he was thrown into a den of lions. God saved Daniel from the lions by sending an angel, who shut the mouths of the lions so they would not hurt Daniel.

There were two men named in the Bible who killed lions. One was a very strong man named Samson, who killed a lion with his bare hands. Another was a shepherd named David, who killed any lion that would try to attack the sheep in his flock.

The Bible also says that there were 12 statues of lions which decorated the steps to King Solomon's throne.

And after a time he returned to take her, and he turned aside to see the carcass of the lion: and, behold, there was a swarm of bees and honey in the carcass of the lion (Isaiah 14:8).

LIZARD

And the ferret, and the chameleon, and the lizard, and the snail, and the mole (Leviticus 11:30).

The lizard was common in Bible lands as it is today. It is found all over the world throughout the warmer climates. Lizards have short legs and scaly skin, and most have long tails. Some lizards' tails separate easily from their bodies. This helps a lizard escape from a predator. If a tail is lost, a new one can be easily grown.

In the Old Testament Book of Leviticus, we learn the lizard was an unclean animal, and it was not to be eaten.

Lizards are interesting animals. They can change color to blend in with the area in which they live. If they live in an area with plants and trees, they will probably be green; if they live in the desert, they will most likely be brown.

The lizard also has movable eyelids, their eardrums on the outside of their body.

LOCUST

The locust is an insect that is similar in appearance to a grasshopper.

The locust is mentioned many times in the Bible. It was very common during Bible times. Locusts caused much damage to crops. God also used locusts as a punishment to Pharaoh and his people, who would not listen to God. Pharaoh did not want to let Moses and the Israelites leave his country, so God sent swarms of locusts into the land (Exodus 10:4). The locusts were so thick that no one could see the ground. They ate trees and crops, filled people's houses, and made life miserable for these people who would not listen to God.

There was one good use for the locust: they could be eaten. The Bible tells us (Leviticus 11:20-21) that any winged insect that hopped could be eaten. This included the locust, the grasshopper, and the cricket. John the Baptist, the man who baptized Jesus, ate locusts with wild honey while he was in the desert (Matthew 3:4).

The locusts have no king, yet go they forth all of them by bands (Proverbs 30:27).

MOLE

In that day a man shall cast his idols of silver, and his idols of gold, which they made each one for himself to worship, to the moles and to the bats (Isaiah 2:20).

The mole is mentioned in the Bible as an unclean animal in the Book of Leviticus. In Bible times there were no true moles living in those areas, and the word mole most likely refers to the mole rat. People who farm or raise crops do not like mole rats. They burrow underneath the ground and ruin crops. They have a pointed nose, which helps them dig through the soil. They do not appear to have eyes, as their eyes are covered with skin. They also do not have ears on the outside of their body.

MOTH

The moth is the second largest order of insect (the beetle is the largest).

The moth is shaped like a butterfly, but does not have the colorful wings of a butterfly. Instead, it has a brownish-looking body and wings. Also, a moth's antennae is not knobbed at the end, while a butterfly's antennae is knobbed.

Moths are destructive insects. They destroy crops and stored items, such as clothing and fabrics. In Bible times fabric was not easy to get, as it was woven by hand. Moths could have easily caused much damage to cloth in those times.

The larvae of the moth is called a caterpillar, and the caterpillar eventually turns into a moth after being in a cocoon.

The Bible cautions us about becoming too interested in collecting material things, because they do not last forever. They can be destroyed by moths, rust, and can be stolen. Only God's love for us lasts forever.

Lay not up for yourselves treasures upon earth, where moth and rust doth corrupt, and where thieves break through and steal (Matthew 6:19).

MOUSE

According to Old Testament law (Leviticus 11:29) the mouse is an unclean animal.

Mice live throughout the world. Some live underground, some live on the ground, and some live in trees. They eat seeds, grasses, and fruits.

In Bible times mice were a big problem, especially because mice would destroy much of the grain crop. Also, homes in Bible times were not tightly sealed as homes are today, and these rodents could easily enter people's homes this way.

There was also no garbage pick up in Bible times as there is today, and rubbish piled up along the streets was likely to attract dogs, mice, rats, and other animals. Mice easily spread disease.

The Bible tells us mice were forbidden as food, but there were some Israelites who did eat them.

MULE

The mule comes from breeding a male donkey and a female horse together. The mule is a strong animal, and is larger than a donkey.

In Bible times the breeding of mules was not allowed by the Jewish people (Leviticus 19:19) because breeding two different kinds of animals was against the Old Testament laws.

Mules were used as pack animals and could easily carry heavy loads. They were also used for transportation, because they are sure-footed. They could easily travel over rocky, mountainous land.

The mule is ridden using a bit and bridle to guide it, just as a horse is ridden.

Be ye not as the horse, or as the mule, which have no understanding: whose mouth must be held in with bit and bridle, lest they come near unto thee (Psalm 32:9).

NIGHTHAWK

In the Old Testament (Deuteronomy 14:15) we find that the nighthawk is an unclean bird, and were not to be eaten.

The nighthawk is a long-winged and long-tailed bird, with a large head and large eyes. It gets its name by flying at night in the dark. It feeds on insects, which it catches at night. It is a speckled black, gray, and tan color.

When nighthawks hunt, they often soar high and dive downwards very quickly, swooping in on their prey.

And the owl, and the night hawk, and the cuckow, and the hawk after his kind (Deuteronomy 14:15).

71

OSPREY

The osprey is a large, fish-eating bird, and is a member of the birds of prey, such as eagles and hawks. In the Old Testament (Leviticus 11:13) the osprey is listed as an unclean bird, not to be eaten.

The osprey lives near the water and feeds on fish. To catch its prey, it glides over the water and swoops down to catch the fish with its powerful talons (claws).

The osprey is dark brown with white on its underside. It builds large nests in trees or in cliffs.

And these are they which ye shall have in abomination among the fowls; they shall not be eaten, they are an abomination: the eagle, and the ossifrage, and the ospray [osprey] (Leviticus 11:13).

OSSIFRAGE

And these are they which ye shall have in abomination among the fowls; they shall not be eaten, they are an abomination: the eagle, and the ossifrage (Leviticus 11:13).

The ossifrage was an unclean animal, according to the Books of Leviticus and Deuteronomy in the Old Testament. It was not used as food for this reason.

The ossifrage is the same bird as the bearded vulture or the lammergeir. The word ossifrage means breaker or bone breaker. This bird drops dead animals from cliffs or other high places. It does this so that the animal's bones will break. This way, with its strong throat muscles, the bird can more easily swallow the smaller pieces of bone, which it eats. This bird is one of the largest vultures known.

OSTRICH

The ostrich is the largest of all birds living today, but it does not fly, even though it has wings and feathers. It can weigh as much as 350 pounds, and is about eight feet tall.

The ostrich is a very quick-running animal. It can reach a speed of about 40 miles per hour. The ostrich likes warm, desert-like climates, which is the climate of the Bible lands.

Ostriches lay their eggs in the sand, but they are easily broken or trampled-on this way. The Bible also tells us the ostrich (Job 39:16) is not a wise bird.

Even the sea monsters draw out the breast, they give suck to their young ones: the daughter of my people is become cruel, like the ostriches in the wilderness (Lamentations 4:3).

OWL

Owls are found all over the world. They have large eyes, but must move their head to see to the left or right. They can turn their head far enough backward to see behind them.

They have soft feathers, large wings, and are a variety of colors: white, brown, tan, and reddish-brown.

Owls are often solitary animals (animals who like to be alone), although burrowing owls and barn owls are frequently found in groups and family bands. They are nocturnal and stay awake to hunt their prey at night. They eat fish, small mammals, insects, and other birds.

The Bible tells us the owl has a sad-sounding voice, is careful of its young, and often lives in deserted cities and houses. It is also an unclean bird, and not to be used as food.

I am like a pelican of the wilderness: I am like an owl of the desert
(Psalm 102:6).

OX

The ox was an important animal in Bible times. It was also a symbol of patience and strength.

In the Bible, the word cattle often referred to the ox. The ox was used as a work animal, but was expensive, so most farmers could only afford to buy a donkey.

The Bible tells us that rich people would eat oxen, and kings would roast it for special occasions, such as for a wedding feast. Sometimes oxen were used for sacrifice (offering) at the altar as a gift to God.

In the New Testament (Luke 13:15) Jesus taught that people should be treated at least as well as oxen.

Oxen were fed on grass, corn, and straw, and were taken to pastures on hills and in valleys.

Oxen were used for pulling wagons, carrying loads, plowing, and treading (crushing) corn with their heavy hoofs.

There were certain laws for using oxen. The Bible tells us that oxen were not to be worked on the Sabbath (the day of worship), and were not to be yoked, or hooked up to a donkey in the same plow. Oxen were also not to be muzzled when treading corn. Also, the fat of the oxen was not to be eaten.

Oxen were also given as presents, and designs of oxen were found in the temple where Jesus worshiped and taught.

Where no oxen are, the crib is clean: but much increase is by the strength of the ox (Proverbs 14:4).

PALMERWORM

The palmerworm is not really a worm, but instead is the young form of a locust, which looks like a worm. When fully grown, the locust looks like a grasshopper.

The palmerworm is not heard of today, and was most likely a name used in earlier times.

In some versions of the Bible, the word "locust" is used instead of palmerworm.

I have smitten you with blasting and mildew: when your gardens and your vineyards and your fig trees and your olive trees increased, the palmerworm devoured them: yet have ye not returned unto me, saith the Lord (Amos 4:9).

PARTRIDGE

The partridge is a bird which is a member of the same group of birds as quails and pheasants. It has rounded wings, but only flies short distances. It has a short beak, which allows it to feed on grain. It lives in a family of other partridges, called a covey, which is made up of parent birds and young or baby birds.

The partridge sits on its eggs but does not hatch them. It lives in desert regions, and still is common in Bible lands today. It's also found in farmlands and grasslands quite abundantly.

As the partridge sitteth on eggs, and hatcheth them not; so he that getteth riches, and not by right, shall leave them in the midst of his days, and his end shall be a fool (Jeremiah 17:11).

PEACOCK

For the king had at sea a navy of Tarshish with the navy of Hiram: once in three years came the navy of Tarshish, bringing gold, and silver, ivory, and apes, and peacocks (1 Kings 10:22).

The peacock is a member of the pheasant family of birds. The male peacock is known for its colorful show of feathers of blue and green. The female peacock — called a peahen — does not have bright colors as the male does.

The peacock has a sharp, high-pitched voice. It eats worms, seeds, insects, and small snakes.

Peacocks were not a native bird to the Bible lands. The Bible tells us they came by cargo ships belonging to King Solomon, who ruled in Bible times.

PELICAN

The pelican is a fish-eating bird and is found in warm climates of the world, and lives near oceans, rivers, and lakes. It feeds on fish. It is a large bird with a very long beak. It has a large pouch-like mouth, which it uses to catch fish. It can store fish in its pouch until it is ready to eat, and its pouch can hold a number of pounds of fish. It also feeds its babies from the fish in its pouch. This bird is also known to gorge itself with fish, and then goes to an isolated place to rest for a few days.

In the Old Testament Book of Leviticus (11:18), the Bible tells us the pelican was unclean and not to be eaten.

And the swan, and the pelican, and the gier eagle
(Leviticus 11:18).

PYGARG

The pygarg is rarely heard of today, but in Bible times was a wild, bearded goat. It is mentioned in the Old Testament as an animal which could be eaten. In many Bibles the phrase wild goat is used instead of pygarg.

The pygarg lives in desert areas and can go for a long time without water. It has wide hoofs, which enables it to walk over sand without sinking. Today it is nearly extinct.

These are the beasts which ye shall eat: the ox, the sheep, and the goat, The hart, and the roebuck, and the fallow deer, and the wild goat, and the pygarg, and the wild ox, and the chamois (Deuteronomy 14:4-5).

QUAIL

The quail is a stout bird which looks like a partridge. In Old Testament times God provided Moses and the people of Israel with quail to eat, as they spent many years traveling through the deserts and needed food. The quail was eaten with manna, which was another type of food God provided for the people to eat. It was a dew-like substance God put on the ground, which the people would collect and then eat (Numbers 11:31-32; Psalm 105:40).

The people asked, and he brought quails, and satisfied them with the bread of heaven
(Psalm 105:40).

Quail feed on insects, grains, and berries. They stay quiet during the day, when they spend time on the ground beneath bushes. They live in families called coveys.

RAM

The ram is a male sheep. It grows strong horns, and in Bible times the horn of a ram was often used as a type of trumpet. Also, skin from these animals was used for the roof of the tabernacle. The tabernacle was a sacred tent that God wanted Moses to build for his people to use for worship.

The mountains skipped like rams, and the little hills like lambs (Psalm 114:4).

In the Old Testament there is a story about a man named Abraham. Abraham loved God very much and obeyed Him. God tested Abraham's faith one day. He asked Abraham to offer his own son, Isaac, as a sacrifice. Just as Abraham was ready to take the knife to offer his son to God, an angel of the Lord called out from heaven to tell Abraham to let the boy go. Abraham then saw a ram caught in a thicket. God had provided the ram for Abraham to use as an offering instead of his son. Abraham was thankful, and God was pleased that Abraham was faithful to Him.

RAVEN

The raven is a large, black bird. It is the largest of all songbirds, and is part of the crow family.

In the Book of Genesis, the raven was the bird that Noah sent out from the ark to see if the flood waters had begun to go down, and the raven is the first bird mentioned in the Bible.

The Bible also tells us that God provides food for the raven: "Consider the ravens: they neither sow nor reap, they have neither storehouse nor barn, and yet God feeds them. Of how much more value are you than the birds!" Ravens eat seeds, small birds, mammals, and fruit.

Who provided for the raven his food? when his young ones cry unto God, they wander for lack of meat (Job 38:41).

In the Bible there is a story about a prophet named Elijah, who had much faith in God. God had told him to go to a certain place by a river, where he was to stay for a long time. God told him to drink the water from the brook so he would not go thirsty, and God provided ravens to bring food for Elijah. Every day Elijah drank water from the brook, and ravens brought him bread and meat every morning and every evening.

SCORPION

The scorpion is found in warm, dry climates. It has a long tail which curves backward over its body when ready to sting. The scorpion stings its prey, and then eats it. It also stings to protect itself. The scorpion's sting is painful and can sometimes cause serious illness or death.

The Bible mentions scorpions a number of times, and they always represent wickedness. Scorpions like warm, dry places, so there were probably many scorpions in the Bible lands.

There is a story in the Bible about Jesus gathering a large number of followers. He sent them out by twos to different cities and towns to spread the Word of God. Jesus gave them power over the serpents and scorpions so that they would not be harmed by them.

Scorpions still live in desert lands today. They are nocturnal, and eat spiders and insects.

SHEEP

Sheep are mentioned over 500 times in the Bible.

The sheep is a tender and loving animal, and it is very dependent upon its shepherd to take care of it. Sheep must be carefully protected, as lions, bears, or wolves can attack and kill them if not guarded.

The shepherd, sometimes hired by the town to watch all the sheep, would keep sheep in a sheepfold (a type of corral) at night to protect them from predators. During the day the shepherd would lead the sheep to green pastures.

Sheep know the voice of their shepherd and listen to him. The sheep can tell a stranger's voice, and will not go with a stranger.

The Bible tells us Jesus is called the "Good Shepherd" (John 10:11). We are His sheep, and He watches over us and cares for us, just as a shepherd watches over his sheep and cares for them.

In Bible times the shepherd often carried a staff, which was a long cane-shaped stick. He would use the staff to guide the sheep, and also used the hooked end of the staff to gather any sheep that wandered away.

The Bible tells us that the shepherd will search and search to find a lost sheep. We know that God cares about us enough that if we are lost or stray from Him, He wants us to come back to Him.

To him the porter openeth; and the sheep hear his voice: and he calleth his own sheep by name, and leadeth them out. And when he putteth forth his own sheep, he goeth before them, and the sheep follow him: for they know his voice (John 10:3-4).

SNAKE

Snakes were common in Bible times. There are different names used to tell about snakes in the Bible. One type of snake is called the adder, which is part of the viper family of snakes. Its bite is very poisonous. Snakes are also sometimes called vipers in the Bible, and are also called serpents in other translations.

The snake is a symbol of evil, and a symbol of the devil (Satan). The Bible tells us that snakes are an unclean animal and are not fit to be eaten. Snakes are also sly or tricky animals.

The Bible tells us many things about snakes: they are cursed above all creatures (Genesis 3:14); they are doomed to creep on their belly all their life (Genesis 3:14); and many kinds are poisonous (Deuteronomy 32:24).

Snakes are also dangerous to travelers, the Bible says, and most people do not like snakes. In Bible times they were often sent as punishment (Numbers 21:6).

Snakes live in hedges, in holes, and in the desert. Their young are hatched from eggs. Snakes eat small animals and rodents.

Deliver me, O Lord, from the evil man: preserve me from the violent man; Which imagine mischiefs in their heart; continually are they gathered together for war. They have sharpened their tongues like a serpent; adders' poison is under their lips (Psalm 140:1-3).

SNAIL

Snails are found all over the world. Some snails live in water or in the ocean, and some live on land. A snail belongs to a group of animals called mollusks. Mollusks have a hard shell as their outside body. A snail carries its shell on its back, and when in danger it keeps its body inside the shell.

In the Bible, in Psalm 58:8, God uses the snail and its slime as an example of what can happen to a wicked person, that "they may be like snails that dissolve into slime."

The soft body beneath the snail's shell is slime-like, and with its one and only foot, it leaves a trail of this slime behind as it travels. A snail travels at a very slow pace. Snails feed on algae and other decaying material. Some oceanic snails actually hunt; they have darts and will shoot fish, paralyze them, then eat them.

As a snail which melteth, let every one of them pass away: like the untimely birth of a woman, [like a stillborn] that they may not see the sun (Psalm 58:8).

Are not two sparrows sold for a farthing? and one of them shall not fall on the ground without your Father. But the very hairs of your head are all numbered. Fear ye not therefore, ye are of more value than many sparrows
(Matthew 10:29-31).

SPARROW

The Bible tells us that God cares even for tiny birds such as sparrows, and that He knows everything that happens to these creatures, even when they fall to the ground.

God tells us we are much more important than sparrows (Matthew 10:29-31). God even knows how many hairs we have on our head.

The sparrow was a common bird in Bible times, and still lives in Bible lands today. It is a small bird with gray/brown feathers. It eats seeds, fruits, and insects on or near the ground, and makes its nest on the ground or in the bushes.

In Bible times, very poor people would give sparrows as an offering to God, since they could not afford sheep or other animals as offerings.

SPIDER

The Bible compares a spider's web with a person who does not believe in God. A spider's web is easily broken, and is not strong, just as a person without faith in God is not strong.

Spiders are found throughout the world, and there are more than 30,000 types of spiders. They can be as small as a dot, or as large as 12 inches across in more exotic locations. They use their webs to trap insects, and they eat their prey alive. Spiders are arthropods: they have eight legs, which are jointed, and segmented bodies. They do not have a spine (they are invertebrates).

Spiders are common in Bible lands, especially poisonous spiders, such as black widows.

So are the paths of all that forget God; and the hypocrite's hope shall perish: Whose hope shall be cut off, and whose trust shall be a spider's web. He shall lean upon his house, but it shall not stand: he shall hold it fast, but it shall not endure (Job 8:13-15).

STORK

The stork is a large bird, usually white and black in color. It has very long legs, webbed toes, and a straight, pointed bill.

In Bible times there was a man named Jeremiah, who was a prophet. Jeremiah noticed what a wise bird the stork is, because it knows when to migrate, that is, it knows when to move from one region of land to another, and at what time of year to do this.

Storks have been known to be kind and wise birds. They live in marshy, swampy places. They eat fish and small mammals. An interesting fact about the stork is that it does not have a voice as an adult. They will produce a hissing sound and they will also rattle their beaks at each other as a sign of noise and recognition, and as a warning.

SWALLOW

A swallow is a bird with long, pointed wings. It is a very strong bird in flight, and it is a migrating bird, spending time in the Bible lands part of the year.

From the Bible verse in Psalm 84:3, we know the swallow is a wise bird, in the way it makes a nest for herself and her young. In Bible times, swallows were known to nest inside the temple.

The swallow feeds on bad bugs such as mosquitoes and gnats. By eating the bad bugs, the swallow helps save crops from being destroyed.

Yea, the sparrow hath found an house, and the swallow a nest for herself, where she may lay her young, even thine altars, O Lord of hosts, my King, and my God (Psalm 84:3).

SWINE

Swine (better known as pigs), were not liked by the Jewish people in Old Testament times. Swine were considered unclean (Leviticus 11:7-8), and the meat from pigs was forbidden to be eaten. The Bible tells us they are filthy animals (2 Peter 22) and the Jewish people did not even want to touch them.

When wild, swine live in wooded areas and can be destructive to crops.

There is a story in the Bible about a young man called the prodigal son. He left his father's home to go to the city, where he foolishly spent all of his money. Soon he was broke and had no more money. The only job he could find was taking care of a herd of dirty pigs, and that was a job that no one liked to do.

Another story in the Bible (Matthew 8:28-32) is about two men with demons. Jesus drove the demons out of the men and into a herd of pigs on a cliff. The pigs rushed over the side of the cliff and were drowned in the water below.

TURTLEDOVE

The turtledove has nothing to do with a turtle, instead it is a type of dove mentioned in the Bible. A dove is a bird that looks much like a pigeon, but is smaller. The dove was often used for sacrifice (offering) to God at the altar during Old Testament times. Poor people who could not afford any other animal for sacrifice would use doves as their offering to God.

In the New Testament (Luke 2:24), the turtledove is spoken of, and was to be offered for sacrifice to God.

The turtledove is also sometimes called a ringed turtledove. It is a pale, tan color, with a ring of black on the back of its neck.

And to offer a sacrifice according to that which is said in the law of the Lord, A pair of turtledoves, or two young pigeons (Luke 2:24).

TORTOISE

In Old Testament times, the tortoise was common. It was, however, an unclean animal, and was not eaten.

Tortoises lives in warm climates. They lay eggs, from which their babies hatch. Some tortoises live as many as 100 years.

Tortoises live on land. There are many types of tortoises, and they come in a variety of sizes and shades of green or brown.

UNICORN

The unicorn is mentioned in some versions of the Bible, but it actually refers to a wild ox. Outside the Bible, the unicorn is a mythical animal, told about in stories, or fairy tales. The unicorn was said to be white, with the head and body of a horse, with one twisting-shaped horn on its head. Bible scholars are not entirely sure of the identity of the biblical unicorn, but it was definitely a real animal. The common interpretation is that this was a wild ox, or possibly a buffalo.

Some wild ox have one horn, and some have two. The Bible tells us this animal was one of great strength (Job 39:11), and was also difficult to catch.

Canst thou bind the unicorn with his band in the furrow? or will he harrow the valleys after thee? (Job 39:10).

VIPER

And when Paul had gathered a bundle of sticks, and laid them on the fire, there came a viper out of the heat, and fastened on his hand (Acts 28:3).

In the Bible, the viper refers to a type of poisonous snake. The head of the viper is wide and triangle-shaped. Its venom (poison) is strong, and affects the blood and tissues of its victim.

There are many types of vipers, and they live mainly in Europe, Africa, and Asia. North and Central America are home to a commonly-feared viper, the rattlesnake.

Snakes in the Bible were also known by the names adder and asp.

Jesus had a disciple named Paul. Paul was on a ship which wrecked at sea, and he ended up on an island called Malta. While on the island one day, he was bitten on the hand by a viper. The native people thought Paul would surely die; however, Paul shook the snake off into the fire and was not hurt. Paul was a man who had much faith in God. The native people believed Paul was a very religious man.

VULTURE

The vulture is an unclean bird according to the Old Testament in the Bible, and was not eaten.

There are a number of different vultures mentioned in the Bible. The most common vulture in Bible lands is the griffon vulture. Another vulture, the lammergeir or bearded vulture, is the largest vulture. This bird is also known as the ossifrage. This bird will drop dead animals from high places in order to crush its bones. This makes it easier for it to to eat these smaller pieces of bones. It has strong throat muscles for eating this type of food. Another vulture is known as the Egyptian vulture, which is the smallest of the vultures.

Vultures live off of dead animals, which is a result of the Fall and the Curse. Before that time, God had provided a perfect world for man.

The Bible tells us that vultures have keen eyesight, and that they are always on the watch for prey.

There shall the great owl make her nest, and lay, and hatch, and gather under her shadow: there shall the vultures also be gathered, every one with her mate (Isaiah 34:15).

WEASEL

The weasel is a small, meat-eating animal, and is related to the ferret. It has a long neck, short legs, and a snake-like body. It is usually brown with a white underside. It is nocturnal, and feeds on mice, rabbits, rats, snakes, grubs, insects, birds, and eggs.

In the Old Testament the weasel was considered an unclean animal, as it was one of the animals that crept upon the earth. The weasel was not a very popular animal in Bible times, and that hasn't changed today! As a matter of fact, weasels are often compared to sneaky people who do things they're not supposed to do. Just as a real weasel will try to steal food, so too, do people sometimes act dishonest.

WHALE

There is a story in the Bible about a prophet named Jonah and a whale. On day, God told Jonah to go to a city called Nineveh, which was filled with wicked people. God wanted Jonah to tell the people in Nineveh that God would destroy their city if they did not stop being wicked.

For as Jonas was three days and three nights in the whale's belly; so shall the Son of man be three days and three nights in the heart of the earth (Matthew 12:40).

Jonah did not obey God. He was afraid, and he ran away to a place called Joppa, where he sailed in a ship headed to Spain. God sent a strong wind out on the ocean, which was dangerous for Jonah and the other sailors. The sailors were angry when they found out that Jonah had run away from God. "It's your fault we had this terrible storm," the sailors told Jonah, so they threw him into the sea, and a great whale swallowed Jonah.

Jonah stayed in the whale's belly for three days and three nights. He was sorry that he had disobeyed God, so God saved him by having the whale spit him out to safety on the shore.

There are other animal names in the Bible which refer to the whale. They are: the sea monster, the dragon, and the great fish.

WOLF

Wolves are mentioned in the Bible as savage and dangerous animals. Wolves were feared by shepherds, who guarded their sheep against them, because wolves would attack and kill sheep for food.

In the Bible, Jesus told His disciples to beware of evil people. He referred to evil people as wolves (Luke 10:3) because they prey on innocent people.

Wolves have powerful teeth. They eat small animals, birds, sheep, and some larger mammals.

Today there are fewer wolves because of the increasing number of people entering their territory. Wolves can't live around people as the coyotes. They have moved to the northern wilderness of the United States and Canada.

WORM

When the word worm is used in the Bible, it is not the same worm that lives in the dirt. Instead, the type of worm spoken about in the Bible is called a maggot, which is the larvae of an insect which looks like a worm.

In Old Testament times, there was a man named Job, who had much faith in God. However, one day Satan (the devil) tested Job's faith by making his life miserable. Job's skin was covered with sores, worms, and dirt. As miserable as Job was, he did not give up. He still had faith in God, and he knew God would take care of him.

In Bible times people believed worms were a form of punishment for things they did wrong.

My flesh is clothed with worms and clods of dust; my skin is broken, and become loathsome
(Job 7:5a).

GLOSSARY

ark — a special boat built by Noah (a man who obeyed God), to protect him, his family, and the animals from the flood that God would send to the earth.

arthropod — means "jointed legs". These include insects, spiders, and scorpions.

Apostle — follower of Jesus who was specially commissioned to teach others about Jesus.

beast — any large animal in the Bible.

betray — to turn against someone.

carnivorous — meat-eating (carnivorous animals who eat other animals).

clean animal — any animal that Old Testament law allowed a person to eat; an animal that did not live in filthy places, or an animal that was not filled with harmful bacteria or parasites.

domestic — having to do with a household or family.

larva — a tiny, wingless animal which hatches from the eggs of insects.

migrate — to move from one country or place to another.

New Testament — all of the books of the Bible that were written after the birth of Jesus.

nocturnal — active at night.

offering — an offering is a gift given to God; for example: money.

Old Testament — all of the books of the Bible which that were written before the birth of Jesus.

parasite — a plant or animal that lives on or in another (host) plant or animal at the expense of the host.

predator — an animal that eats or lives off of other animals.

prophet — a person who has been given special knowledge or power from God.

sacrifice — an animal that was given for sacrifice was an animal that was killed and given to God as a gift (offering).

shepherd — a person who takes care of sheep.

tabernacle — a sacred tent built by Moses and his people for worshiping God.

temple — a place of worship where Jesus taught.

tropical — the area just north and south of the equator which contains rain forests and dry deserts.

unclean animal — any animal in the Bible which was said by Old Testament law to be unclean; an animal that lived in filthy places, or an animal that had harmful bacteria or parasites.

venom — the poison that comes from snakes, spiders, insects and other animals.

wealthy — having a lot of money or things.